STARS in the SPOTLIGHT

Orlando Bloom

Colleen Adams

PowerKiDS
press™

New York

Published in 2007 by The Rosen Publishing Group, Inc.
29 East 21st Street, New York, NY 10010

Book Design: Haley Wilson

Photo Credits: Cover © Giulio Marcocchi/Getty Images; p. 4 © Filippo Monteforte/AFP/Getty Images; pp. 6, 8, 18, 26 © Dave Hogan/Getty Images; pp. 10, 14 © Kevin Winter/Getty Images; p. 12 © Sion Touhig/Getty Images; p. 16 © Anthony Harvey/Getty Images; pp. 20, 22, 28 © Evan Agostini/Getty Images; p. 24 © Pascal Le Segretain/Getty Images.

Library of Congress Cataloging-in-Publication Data

Adams, Colleen.
  Orlando Bloom / Colleen Adams.
      p. cm. — (Stars in the spotlight)
  Includes index.
  ISBN-13: 978-1-4042-3517-5
  ISBN-10: 1-4042-3517-5 (library binding)
  1. Bloom, Orlando, 1977—Juvenile literature. 2. Motion picture actors and actresses—Great Britain—Biography—Juvenile literature. I. Title. II. Series.
  PN2598.B6394A33 2007
  791.4302'8'092—dc22
  [B]
                            2006017780

Manufactured in the United States of America

Contents

4

An Action Hero

Orlando Bloom is a well-known actor who has played many roles in action-adventure movies. He dreamed of being an actor at a young age. Orlando moved to London, England, when he was 16 and joined the National Youth Theatre. He landed the role of Legolas in the three *The Lord of the Rings* movies in 1999. In order to play Legolas and other action characters, Orlando learned to shoot a bow and arrows, sword fight, and ride horseback. He has earned the respect of other actors and fans for his performances in *Troy*, *Kingdom of Heaven*, and the *Pirates of the Caribbean* movies.

Orlando signs autographs for fans in Italy in 2005.

6

Growing Up

Orlando Jonathan Blanchard Bloom was born in Canterbury, England, on January 13, 1977. His father, Harry Bloom, fought for **civil rights** in South Africa. Sadly, he died when Orlando was only 4 years old. Orlando lived with his mother, Sonia Copeland, and his older sister, Samantha. School was difficult for Orlando because he had **dyslexia**. He liked making pottery and taking pictures. He also acted in school plays and was involved in local theater. Orlando and Samantha often won poetry reading contests as well. Orlando decided he wanted to be an actor. He moved to London when he was 16 to join the National Youth Theatre.

Orlando poses with his mom, Sonia (left), and his sister, Samantha (right), in 2005.

8

Acting School

Orlando spent 2 years at the National Youth Theatre. He later earned a **scholarship** to the British American Drama Academy in London. Orlando **auditioned** for and took small parts on television shows to gain acting experience. He also got a small role in a movie in 1997. Orlando attended the Guildhall School of Music and Drama for 3 years.

While Orlando was a student at Guildhall, he fell three stories from a rooftop and broke his back. Doctors thought that he would not be able to walk again. Luckily, he was able to recover quickly. Orlando was happy to get back to acting once again.

Orlando appeared in many plays, such as *Twelfth Night* and *The Seagull*, while he attended the Guildhall School of Music and Drama.

10

Orlando Gets Discovered

One night in 1999, a director named Peter Jackson saw Orlando in a play. Jackson asked Orlando to audition for a part in *The Lord of the Rings* movies he was directing. Orlando did, and Jackson offered him the role of an elf named Legolas. Orlando accepted the offer shortly after graduating from Guildhall. He went to New Zealand to work on the first movie, *The Lord of the Rings: The **Fellowship** of the Ring*. After his performances in these movies, Orlando became a well-known actor.

Orlando got his big break as an actor when he was offered the role of Legolas in *The Lord of the Rings* movies.

The Fellowship of the Ring

The Lord of the Rings movies were based on books by J. R. R. Tolkien. In *The Fellowship of the Ring,* **hobbit** Frodo Baggins and his gardener, Sam, set out on a long journey. Frodo must destroy the One Ring, the most powerful of the Rings of Power, which was left to him by his cousin Bilbo. If the evil lord Sauron gets the ring, he will use it to destroy everything good in Middle-earth. Frodo has to take the ring to Mount Doom in Sauron's kingdom, the only place it can be destroyed. Frodo and Sam are joined by the fellowship of the ring, a group of characters who guide them and help them reach their goal.

Orlando is shown with actors Elijah Wood and Liv Taylor, who worked with him on *The Lord of the Rings* movies.

Legolas

In *The Lord of the Rings* movies, Legolas is an elf **warrior** with a talent for archery. He is chosen to represent the elves in the fellowship of the ring because he is strong and loyal. Others in the fellowship include Gandalf the Wizard; the hobbits Merry, Pippin, and Sam; Gimli the dwarf; Boromir of Gondor; and a tall stranger named Strider, whose true name is Aragorn. Legolas helps to protect Frodo and the fellowship as they go to destroy the One Ring. The fellowship encounters many problems along the way. *The Two Towers* and *The Return of the King* tell the rest of the story.

Orlando is shown here with actor Viggo Mortensen, who played Aragorn in *The Lord of the Rings* movies.

15

Black Hawk Down

After he finished filming *The Lord of the Rings* movies, Orlando moved to Los Angeles, California, in 2001. He was chosen for a small role in the movie *Black Hawk Down*. This true story is about a 1993 U.S. Army **mission** in Somalia, Africa. The mission ended in a battle that killed and wounded many American soldiers. Orlando plays a young private who breaks his back falling from a helicopter. He received good reviews for his performance and gained more respect as an actor. As a result, he was offered more roles in movies.

After *Black Hawk Down*, Orlando took a role in a movie about an Australian outlaw called *Ned Kelly*.

17

Pirates of the Caribbean

Orlando played the role of Will Turner in the 2003 movie *Pirates of the Caribbean: The Curse of the Black Pearl*. Will is a young man who secretly loves his childhood friend Elizabeth Swann. Elizabeth is captured by the wicked Captain Barbossa and his crew of dangerous pirates. Will and Captain Jack Sparrow team up to go after Barbossa and save Elizabeth. Will, Captain Jack, and Elizabeth then take part in an adventure that leads them to the truth about the *Black Pearl* pirate ship and the discovery of lost treasure.

Orlando and Keira Knightley, who played Elizabeth Swann, are shown at the opening of *Pirates of the Caribbean: The Curse of the Black Pearl* in 2003.

Troy

In 2003, Orlando worked on another action film called *Troy*. It was based on a famous ancient Greek poem about the Trojan War, a conflict between the ancient cities of Troy and Sparta. One main character is Hector, the leader of the Trojan army. Orlando played the role of Paris, Hector's younger brother. Paris falls in love with the beautiful Helen and takes her away from her husband, Menelaus, the king of Sparta. This event starts a war that lasts for 10 years. In the end, Paris loses everything by making foolish mistakes. This movie featured many well-known actors, including Brad Pitt as the Greek warrior Achilles.

Orlando costarred with Eric Bana (left) as Hector and Brad Pitt (middle) as Achilles in *Troy*.

Kingdom of Heaven

Orlando got his first starring movie role in 2005. The movie, *Kingdom of Heaven*, is set in Europe and the Middle East during the twelfth century. Orlando plays Balian, a young blacksmith. Balian is mourning the loss of his family when he is asked to go to Jerusalem. Once he is there, Balian earns the respect of the people. He becomes a knight and fights against **invaders**. As a brave leader, he struggles to protect the people of Jerusalem and keep peace during a difficult time in history.

Orlando is shown with actors Liam Neeson and Eva Green at the New York City opening of *Kingdom of Heaven*.

Elizabethtown

In 2005, Orlando starred in *Elizabethtown*. In this movie, Orlando doesn't have a bow and arrows or a horse. He plays a modern-day character named Drew Baylor. Drew's life changes when he loses his job. Then he is told that his father has died suddenly. Drew is sad when he travels to his family's home in the small town of Elizabethtown, Kentucky. He learns a lot about himself while he is visiting. Drew learns to face his problems with the help of his family and a new friend.

Orlando and costars Susan Sarandon (left) and Kirsten Dunst (right) pose for a picture at the opening of *Elizabethtown*.

Pirates of the Caribbean: Dead Man's Chest

In 2006, Orlando starred in a **sequel** called *Pirates of the Caribbean: Dead Man's Chest*. This time Will, Elizabeth, and Captain Jack Sparrow are caught up in an adventure with **supernatural** warriors. Captain Jack learns he must settle a debt with Davey Jones, the captain of the ghost ship the *Flying Dutchman*. Jack only has a short amount of time to save himself, or he will be forced to serve Jones in the **afterlife**. Elizabeth and Will delay their wedding plans and rush to help Jack.

Orlando appears in a third *Pirates of the Caribbean* movie due out in 2007.

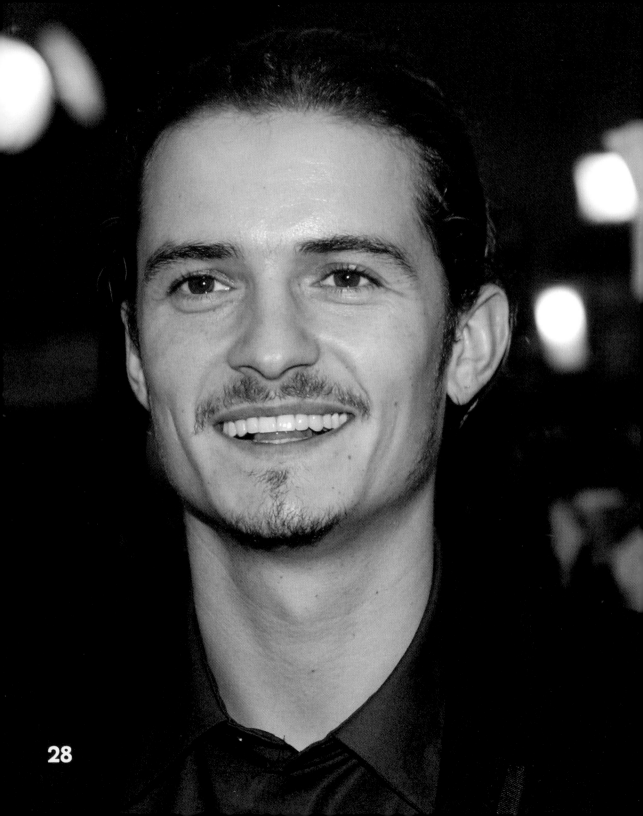

"Global Warming Isn't Cool"

Orlando has joined famous people such as Mischa Barton and Kevin Bacon in a poster campaign for ClimateStar.org. This campaign informs people about the dangers of **global warming**. It also suggests things everyone can do to help stop it. Each poster addresses an issue related to the **environment**. On his poster, Orlando tells us that the results of global warming include frequent heat waves, increased air pollution, and the spread of diseases. Some of the suggestions for preventing global warming include planting new trees, using energy wisely, and joining a car pool.

Orlando supports the ClimateStar.org campaign to stop global warming. Each poster ends with the slogan "Global warming isn't cool. Stopping it is."

29

Orlando's Plans

Orlando's hard work and love of acting have made his childhood dreams come true. His formal training as an actor started on stage. Maybe someday Orlando will return to the stage. He has been invited to perform with the Royal Shakespeare Company in the English city of Stratford-upon-Avon. Orlando said that he would love to take on the role of Hamlet, one of Shakespeare's most difficult characters to play. He plans to perform with the group when he has a break from making movies. In the meantime, we can look forward to seeing Orlando in movies for many years to come.

Glossary

afterlife (AF-tuhr-lyf) Existence after death.

audition (aw-DIH-shun) To take part in a performance that tests the ability of an actor, singer, musician, or dancer.

civil rights (SIH-vuhl RYTS) The rights of a citizen. Civil rights are sometimes wrongly kept from some groups of people.

dyslexia (dihs-LEHK-see-uh) A learning disability that involves problems with reading, writing, and spelling. A person with dyslexia may see and write letters and numbers backwards.

environment (ihn-VY-ruhn-muhnt) Everything that surrounds a living thing and affects its growth and health.

fellowship (FEH-loh-ship) A group of people who share the same interests or goals.

global warming (GLOH-buhl WOHR-ming) An increase in Earth's temperatures that results from air pollution.

hobbit (HAH-buht) A make-believe small humanlike creature invented by author J. R. R. Tolkien. Hobbits have hairy feet, live underground, and are peaceful.

invader (ihn-VAY-duhr) One who enters a place by force to free or conquer.

mission (MIH-shun) A special job or task given to a person or group of people.

scholarship (SKAH-luhr-ship) Money given to a student to pay for education.

sequel (SEE-kwuhl) A book or story that is complete in itself but continues a story begun in an earlier work.

supernatural (soo-puhr-NA-chuh-ruhl) Having to do with forces separate from or higher than the laws of nature.

warrior (WOHR-yuhr) A person who fights or has experience in battle.

Index

Web Sites

Due to the changing nature of Internet links, PowerKids Press has developed an online list of Web sites related to the subject of this book. This site is updated regularly. Please use this link to access the list:
http://www.powerkidslinks.com/stars/bloom/